INCREASE YOUR WEALTH WITH AI

Copyright 2023

ISBN   9798862557794

Contents

6

INTRODUCTION

In an era where technology reigns supreme and the pace of change is unprecedented, the convergence of artificial intelligence (AI) and wealth creation has emerged as a transformative force. "Increase Your Wealth With AI" is not just a book; it's your roadmap to navigating the dynamic landscape of the modern economy, empowering you to harness the potential of AI to amplify your financial prosperity.

The traditional paradigms of wealth accumulation are being reshaped by the integration of AI into every facet of our lives. From optimizing investment strategies and predicting market trends to automating business processes and uncovering hidden opportunities, AI has transcended its role as a mere tool. It has become the catalyst that propels those who understand its capabilities and intricacies to new heights of financial success.

In this book we delve into the synergies between AI and wealth generation, demystifying complex concepts and illustrating how even the most novice of individuals can leverage AI to unlock doors previously thought to be accessible only to financial experts. Whether you're an entrepreneur aiming to revolutionize your industry, an investor seeking the edge in an ever competitive market or simply someone who wants to secure a prosperous future, the insights within these pages will be your guiding light.

We'll embark on a journey that encompasses not only the technical aspects of AI but also the mindset shift required to fully embrace its transformative potential. Moreover, we'll adress the ethical considerations inherent in this AI powered financial landscape, ensuring that your pursuit of wealth aligns with broader societal values.

Whether you're an AI novice or a seasoned technophile, "Increase Your Weath With AI" is designed to equip you with actionable insights, practical strategies and a comprehensive understanding of how AI can be wielded as a tool for financial prosperity. The future is here and the time to seize its opportunities is now. So buckle up and prepare to embark on a transformative journey that will reshape the way you think about wealth, AI and the boundless possibilities that lie ahead.

8

Let's get down to business and look at some ideas that leverage the power of AI:

AI-Powered Personalized Marketing

Develop an AI driven marketing platform that analyzes consumer behaviour, preferences and online interactions to create highly personalized marketing campaigns.This could involve sending tailored recommendations, offers and content to individuals, thereby increasing engagement and conversion rates for businesses.

In today's fast-paced digital world, businesses are constantly seeking innovative ways to connect with their target audiences and drive meaningful engagement. The advent of AI has revolutionized the marketing landscape, offering the potential to create highly personalized marketing campaigns that resonate with individual consumers. Let's explore the intricate process of developing an AI-driven platform that analyzes consumer behaviour, preferences and online interactions to craft tailored marketing strategies. By harnessing the power of AI, businesses can gain deeper insights into their customers, enhance brand loyalty and ultimately achieve higher conversion rates.

Understanding Consumer Behaviour and Preferences

At the heart of any successful marketing campaign lies a profound understanding of consumer behaviour and preferences. AI offers the tools to gather, analyze and interpret vast amounts of data from various sources including social media, online purchases, search history and more. Machine learning algorithms can identify patterns and trends within this data, unveiling valuable insights into what drives consumer decision making. For instance, AI can discern which products or services consumers are searching for, which features they prioritize and what influences their purchasing decisions.

Data Collection and Integration

The first step in developing an AI driven marketing platform is to establish a robust data collection process.This involves gathering data from multiple touchpoints, such as websites, mobile apps, social media platforms and email interactions. Advanced data integration techniques are employed to consolidate this data into a centralized repository, providing a holistic view of consumer behaviour. The collected data encompasses demographic information, browsing history, transaction records and even sentiment analysis derived from online interactions.

Machine Learning and Predictive Analytics

Once the data is aggregated, machine learning algorithms come into play. These algorithms use historical data to train models that can predict future consumer behaviour and preferences. Predictive analytics enable marketers to anticipate customer needs and tailor marketing messages accordingly. For example, a clothing retailer can predict upcoming fashion trends based on previous buying patterns and social media trends, allowing them to develop timely and relevant campaigns.

Segmentation and Personalization

Segmentation is a crucial component of personalized marketing. AI can categorize consumers into distinct segments based on shared characteristics, behaviours and preferences. These segments are then used to create tailored marketing messages that resonate with each group. For instance, an e-commerce platform can segment its audience into categories such as "frequent shoppers", "budget-conscious buyers" or "luxury enthusiasts". AI-powered platforms can then craft marketing content specific to each segment, optimizing the chances of engagement and conversion.

Real-time Campaign Optimization

The dynamic nature of the online environment calls for real-time campaign optimization. AI-equipped platforms continuously monitor consumer interactions and responses to marketing initiatives. Through real-time analysis the system can identify which campaigns are resonating with specific segments and which are falling flat. This iterative process allows marketers to adjust their strategies on the fly, reallocating resources to the most effective campaigns and refining their approach to maximize inpact.

Natural Language Processing (NLP) for Content Creation

A pivotal act of personalized marketing is the creation of compelling content. Natural Language Processing (NLP) technologies enable AI systems to generate written content that aligns with each segment's preferences. By analyzing the language, tone and style that resonate with different audience segments, AI can craft personalized email messages, media posts and even blog articles.This level of customization enhances the user experience and fosters a deeper connection between consumers and brands.

Ethical Considerations and Data Privacy

While the potential benefits of AI-driven personalized marketing are immense, it's imperative to address ethical considerations and data privacy. Collecting and analyzing consumer data must be conducted transparently and with the explicit consent of users. Data security measures should be implemented to safeguard sensitive information.

Moreover, AI algorithms should be designed to avoid reinforcing biases and to ensure fair treatment across all demographic groups.

Conclusion

The development of an AI-driven platform that analyzes consumer behaviour, preferences and online interactions to create highly personalized marketing campaigns represents a significant stride in the evolution of modern marketing strategies. Through meticulous data collection, machine learning and real-time optimization, businesses can establish a deeper connection with their audience, resulting in increased engagement and conversion rates. However, it's crucial to approach this technology ethically, respecting user privacy and avoiding algorithmic biases. As AI technology continues to evolve, the potential to create truly personalized marketing experiences is bound to reshape the way brands and consumers interact in the digital age.

Leveraging AI-Driven Customer Service for Profitable Business Growth

In today's competitive business landscape, customer service has emerged as a crucial factor that can set companies apart. With the rapid advances in AI, businesses are discovering innovative ways to enhance their customer service offerings and in turn boost profitability. I will now delve into the strategies and benefits of using an AI-driven customer service platform to generate revenue, improve customer satisfaction and drive sustainable business growth.

The Evolution of Customer Service

Traditionally, customer service has involved human interactions, often through call centers or email support. However this model can be labor intensive, time consuming and prone to inconsistencies in response quality. AI has ushered in a new era of customer service by introducing automation, personalization and efficiency. AI-driven customer service platforms utilize technologies like Natural Language Processing (NLP) and Machine Learning (ML) to understand and respond to customer queries, offering real-time solutions and a seamless user experience.

Cost Reduction and Efficiency Gains

One of the most compelling ways AI-driven customer service platforms contribute to a business's profitability is through cost reduction and operational efficiency. With AI-powered chatbots and virtual assistants, businesses can handle a substantial portion of routine customer inquiries without human intervention. This leads to significant savings on labor costs as fewer human agents are required to address basic issues. Moreover, AI operates 24/7, providing round-the-clock support to customers around the globe without the limitations of human working hours.

Enhanced Customer Satisfaction

Happy customers are loyal customers and AI-driven customer service can significantly enhance customer satisfaction levels. By providing instant responses and resolving issues in real time, businesses can meet customers' expectations for swift and effective suport. AI platforms can also track customer interactions and preferences over time, enabling personalized recommendations and tailored responses. This level of individualized attention fosters a sense of value and connection, ultimately leading to increased customer loyalty and repeat business.

Cross-Selling and Upselling Opportunities

AI-driven customer service platforms possess the capability to analyze customer interactions and purchase history, enabling businesses to identify cross-selling and upselling opportunities. By understanding customers' preferences and needs, AI can suggest relevant products or services that align with their interests. For instance, an e-commerce platform can use AI to recommend complementary items based on a customer's recent purchase, leading to higher average order values and increased revenue per customer.

Data-Driven Insights for Business Strategy

The data generated by AI-driven customer service interactions is a goldmine of insights that can inform strategic decision making. By analyzing patterns in customer inquiries, businesses can identify pain points, recurring issues and areas for improvement in their products or services. This feedback loop enables businesses to refine their offerings, enhance customer experiences and proactively address potential concerns. Informed business strategies lead to increased customer satisfaction and ultimately greater profitablity.

Customized Marketing and Targeted Campaigns

AI-driven customer service platforms can contribute to revenue generation beyond the support function. By analyzing customer preferences, behaviour and historical interactions, businesses can craft personalized marketing messages and targeted campaigns. For example, an AI platform could identify customers who have shown interest in a specific product but haven't made a purchase. These customers could be targeted with exclusive offers or promotions, increasing the likelihood of conversion and boosting sales.

Continuous Improvement through Machine Learning

AI-powered customer service platforms continuously learn and adapt through machine learning algorithms. As these systems interact with more customers over time, they become increasingly proficient at understanding context, delivering accurate responses and handling complex queries. This iterative learning process translates to higher accuracy rates, fewer errors and improved customer experiences, which in turn lead to positive word-of-mouth referrals and repeat business.

Building Brand Reputation and Trust

Exceptional customer service contributes significantly to building a strong brand reputation and fostering trust among customers. AI-driven platforms can provide consistent and reliable support, ensuring that customers receive the same level of assistance regardless of the time of day. When customers feel valued and heard, they are more likely to recommend the brand to others and become brand advocates. This organic promotion can lead to a larger customer base and consequently increased revenue.

Conclusion

The integration of AI-driven customer service platforms represents a transformative shift in the way businesses can generate revenue and improve profitability. Through cost savings, enhanced customer satisfaction, cross-selling opportunities, data-driven insights and personalized marketing, businesses can unlock a multitude of benefits that contribute to their bottom line. While AI augments the customer service landscape, it's crucial to strike a balance between automation and the human touch, ensuring that customers always have access to the level of support they require. In a digital age where customer experience reigns supreme, leveraging AI-driven customer service is not just a strategy for revenue generation but a pathway to sustainable growth and competitive advantage.

Creating an AI-Based Financial Advisory Service: A Path to Informed Decision Making

In an increasingly complex and dynamic financial landscape, individuals and businesses seek sound guidance to navigate investment opportunities, manage risks and secure their financial futures. The emergence of AI has revolutionized the financial advisory sector by offering data-driven insights, predictive analytics and personalized recommendations. In this chapter we will delve into the intricate process of creating an AI-based financial advisory service, exploring the components, benefits and considerations involved in harnessing AI to empower clients with informed decision making in their financial endeavors.

Understanding the Need for AI-Based Financial Advisory

Conventional financial advisory services have traditionally relied on human expertise but they often face limitations in analyzing vast data sets, identifying nuanced market trends and adapting to rapidly changing market conditions. AI addresses these limitations by processing massive amounts of data, recognizing patterns and making data-driven predictions. This level of analysis enables financial advisors and clients to make more informed and timely decisions, enhancing the potential for achieving financial goals.

Data Collection and Aggregation

The foundation of an AI-based financial advisory service lies in comprehensive data collection and aggregation. Relevant financial data, economic indicators, market trends and historical performance metrics are collected from diverse sources such as stock exchanges, financial news outlets, regulatory filings and economic reports. This data forms the raw material that AI algorithms use to generate insights and recommendations.

Machine Learning and Predictive Analytics

Machine Learning (ML) algorithms are at the heart of an AI-based financial advisory service. These algorithms are trained on historical data to recognize patterns, correlations and trends in financial markets. Over time, the algorithms become adept at predicting potential market movements, identifying investment opportunities and assessing risk levels. Predictive analytics enable advisors to offer clients forecasts on asset performance, helping them make more informed investment decisions.

Risk Assessment and Portfolio Optimization

AI-driven financial advisory services excel in assessing risk and optimizing investment portfolios. These services can calculate risk profiles based on client preferences, risk tolerance and financial goals. By analyzing historical data and simulating potential scenarios, AI algorithms can recommend portfolio allocations that maximize returns while minimizing risk. This level of customization allows clients to achieve a balanced portfolio that aligns with their individual financial objectives.

Personalized Recommendations and Insights

One of the key strengths in AI financial advisory lies in its ability to deliver personalized recommendations and insights. AI algorithms can take into account a client's financial history, investment preferences and risk tolerance to provide tailored investment strategies.This personalization enhances the client experience as advice is matched with their specific circumstances and objectives. For instance, AI can recommend diversified investments for risk-averse clients or growth oriented options for those seeking higher returns.

Real-Time Monitoring and Alerts

AI-based financial advisory services offer real-time monitoring of financial markets, which is crucial in today's fast paced trading environment. These services can track market news, stock price movements and global economic events, providing timely alerts to clients who are thus empowered to make swift decisions in response to market developments, optimizing their investment positions and capitalizing on emerging opportunities.

Ethical Considerations and Transparency

While the potential benefits of AI-based financial advisory are significant, ethical considerations and transparency must be prioritized. Clients must have a clear understanding of how AI algorithms generate recommendations and predictions. Moreover, algorithmic biases must be addressed to ensure fair treatment across diverse demographic groups. Data privacy and security are also paramount; robust measures must be in place to protect sensitive financial information and prevent unauthorized access.

Human-AI Collaboration

Creating an AI-based financial advisory service does not entail the complete replacement of human advisors. Rather, it emphasizes a collaborative approach where AI augments human expertise. Human advisors bring nuanced judgement, emotional intelligence and the ability to contextualize complex situations that AI might not fully grasp. The synergy between AI-driven insights and human interpretation leads to more holistic, well informed financial advisory services.

Educational Resources and Empowerment

An essential aspect of AI-based financial advisory is the educational component it provides to clients. Clients can gain a deeper understanding of investment strategies, risk factors and financial concepts through interactive AI-driven tools. These tools can simulate different investment scenarios and demonstrate the potential outcomes, enabling clients to make informed decisions aligned with their financial aspirations.

Conclusion

The advent of AI has transformed the financial advisory landscape, offering a new paradigm that combines data-driven insights, predictive analytics and personalized recommendations. Creating an AI-based financial advisory service involves assembling vast datasets, employing machine learning algorithms and ensuring ethical considerations are met. By harnessing the power of AI, financial advisory services can provide clients with accurate forecasts, optimal portfolio strategies and personalized advice that empowers them to navigate the compexities of the financial world. The future of financial advisory lies in the seamless collaboration between human expertise and AI-driven insights, leading to more informed decision making and better financial outcomes.

Transforming Healthcare: The Business Potential of Algorithms in Diagnostics and Prediction

The healthcare industry stands on the brink of a technological revolution and AI is poised to play a pivotal role in reshaping its landscape. In recent years, AI algorithms have demonstrated remarkable capabilities in healthcare diagnostics and prediction, offering unprecedented accuracy and efficiency in disease detection, prognosis and treatment planning. Here I will explore the compelling reasons why developing AI algorithms in healthcare diagnostics and prediction represents a highly promising business idea. By harnessing the power of AI, businesses can tap into a growing market, improve patient outcomes and contribute to the advancement of medical science.

Enhanced Diagnostic Accuracy

One of the most compelling benefits of AI algorithms in healthcare is their ability to enhance diagnostic accuracy. AI-powered algorithms can analyze vast amounts of medical data, including medical images, patient record and genetic information, with incredible speed and precision. This enables earlier detection of diseases, accurate identification of anomalies and differentiation of complex patterns that might be challenging for human clinicians to discern. By reducing diagnostic errors, AI contributes to more effective and timely interventions, ultimately improving patient outcomes.

Reduced Workload on Healthcare Professionals

AI algorithms can serve as invaluable tools for healthcare professionals by reducing their workload and allowing them to focus on critical decision making tasks. Routine tasks such as reviewing medical images, interpreting test results and data analysis can be automated, freeing up valuable time for physicians and radiologists to concentrate on patient care and complex cases. This enhanced efficiency not only benefits healthcare providers but also ensures that patients receive more comprehensive and attentive medical attention.

Predictive Analytics for Proactive Healthcare

The predictive capabilities of AI are particularly promising for healthcare. By analyzing historical patient data and considering various factors such as genetics, lifestyle and environmental influences, AI can predict the likelihood of disease development and progression. This empowers clinicians to take a proactive approach to healthcare, identifying high risk patients and implementing preventive measures before conditions worsen. Such interventions not only save lives but also contribute to reduced healthcare costs by avoiding expensive emergency treatments.

Personalized Treatment Strategies

AI algorithms enable the creation of highly personalized treatment strategies tailored to individual patients. By considering a patient's medical history, genetic makeup and response to previous treatments, AI can recommend the most suitable therapeutic options. This customization minimizes the risk of adverse rections to treatments and maximizes the chances of treatment success. Developing AI algorithms that facilitate personalized medicine not only benefits patients but also enhances a healthcare business's reputation for delivering superior care.

Efficiency and Cost Savings

Implementing AI algorithms in healthcare diagnostics and prediction can lead to substantial cost savings. Faster and more accurate diagnoses reduce the need for unnecessary tests and procedures, which in turn lowers healthcare expenditures. Additionally, AI streamlines administrative tasks, optimizing resource allocation and increasing operational efficiency. As healthcare costs continue to rise, AI-driven solutions that deliver cost effective and high quality care become increasingly attractive to healthcare providers, insurers and patients alike.

Emerging Market Opportunities

The demand for AI-driven healthcare solutions is on the rise, creating ample market opportunities for businesses. As AI technology matures and gains acceptance in the medical community, there is a growing need for innovative algorithms that can tackle complex diagnostic challenges. Startups and established companies can capitalize on this demand by developing and offering AI-driven diagnostic tools to hospitals, clinics and research institutions. A successful entry into this market can lead to substantial growth and profitability, particularly in the long term as AI becomes an integral part of healthcare.

Research Collaboration and Advancement

The development of AI algorithms in healthcare diagnostics and prediction is not only a business opportunity but also a chance to contribute to scientific advancement. Collaboration with medical professionals and researchers can lead to the creation of cutting-edge algorithms that have the potential to revolutionize patient care. Businesses that invest in research and development partnerships can position themselves as leaders in the field, driving both innovation and progress while reaping the benefits of a strong brand reputation.

Ethical Considerations and Regulatory Compliance

While the potential benefits of AI in healthcare are substantial, ethical considerations and regulatory compliance are of utmost importance. AI algorithms must be developed and deployed in a manner that respects patient privacy, ensures data security and avoids bias. Regulatory bodies such as the Food and Drug Administration (FDA) in the United States, have stringent guidelines for medical AI applications. Businesses that prioritize ethical practices and comply with regulations can build trust with healthcare professionals and patients, facilitating the adoption of their AI solutions.

Conclusion

Developing AI algorithms in healthcare diagnostics and prediction represents a compelling and timely business idea with far reaching benefits. The potential to improve diagnostic accuracy, personalize treatment strategies and foster proactive healthcare presents a remarkable opportunity for businesses to enter a burgeoning market. As AI technology continues to evolve, companies that invest in research, collaborate with healthcare professionals and adhere to ethical and regulatory standards are poised to drive innovation, make a significant impact on patient care and achieve substantial success in the dynamic landscape of healthcare. Ultimately, the integration of AI algorithms in healthcare signifies not only a wise business choice but also a commitment to advancing medical science for the betterment of society.

Revolutionizing Business Operations: The Benefits of AI-Powered Supply Chain Optimization

In the modern global marketplace, efficient supply chain management is critical for businesses to remain competitive and meet customer demands. As businesses strive to streamline operations, reduce costs and enhance customer satisfaction, the integration of AI has emerged as a transformative solution. AI-powered supply chain optimization offers a data-driven approach that revolutionizes traditional practices, providing businesses with unparalleled insights, predictive capabilities and automation opportunities. Here I will lay out the myriad benefits that AI-powered supply chain optimization brings to businesses, ranging from cost savings to improved decision making and increased operational efficiency.

Real-time Data Analysis and Decision Making

One of the central advantages of AI-powered supply chain optimization is the ability to process and analyze massive volumes of real-time data. From demand forecasting and inventory levels to production rates and transportation routes, AI algorithms can synthesize complex data sets and provide businesses with up-to-the-minute insights. This real-time analysis empowers decision makers with accurate information, enabling them to make informed choices promptly. As a result, businesses can respond swiftly to changes in demand, supply disruptions or market shifts, reducing potential risks and maximizing opportunities.

Enhanced Demand Forecasting

AI-driven supply chain optimization greatly enhances demand forecasting accuracy. By analyzing historical data, market trends and external factors such as economic indicators and seasonal variations, AI algorithms can generate precise predictions of future demand. Businesses can then align their production schedules, inventory levels and distribution plans accordingly, minimizing stockouts and excess inventory. Accurate demand forecasting not only improves resource allocation but also leads to higher customer satisfaction, ensuring products are readily available when needed.

Reduced Operational Costs

AI-powered supply chain optimization has a direct impact on cost reduction across various aspects of the supply chain. By optimizing inventory levels, businesses can avoid overstocking, thereby reducing storage costs and the risk of obsolescence. Moreover, efficient route optimization for transportation leads to fuel savings and decreased transportation expenses. Minimizing production downtime through predictive maintenance also contibutes to cost savings. Overall, AI-driven optimization techniques help businesses allocate resources more efficiently, resulting in substantial operational cost reductions.

Inventory Management Efficiency

Effective inventory management is a corner stone of a well functioning supply chain. AI algorithms excel in analyzing historical data and patterns to optimize inventory levels. By considering factors such as lead times, demand fluctuations and order cycle times, AI can recommend optimal reorder points and quantities, This prevents overstocking, stockouts and the associated costs, while ensuring products are available to meet customer demands. Businesses can maintain leaner inventory levels without compromising surface levels, ultimately leading to improved cash flow and reducing holding costs.

Mitigation of Supply Chain Risks

Supply chain disruptions can have severe consequences for businesses, leading to delays, increased costs and reputational damage. AI-powered supply chain optimization enhances risk management by identifying potential vulnerabilities and proposing contingency plans. AI algorithms can monitor external factors such as geopolitical events, natural disasters or supplier issues, to provide early warnings and alternative solutions. Businesses that prioritize risk mitigation through AI-powered insights can navigate unforseen challenges more effectively and ensure business continuity.

Optimized Supplier Relationships

AI-driven supply chain optimization fosters stronger relationships with suppliers. By analyzing supplier performance data, lead times and quality metrics, businesses can identify reliable and efficient partners. Negotiations can be informed by AI insights, ensuring favorable terms while maintaining the quality of goods and services. This collaborative approach to supply management improves communication, reduces lead times and enhances overall supply chain efficiency.

Sustainable Practices

In an era of increasing environmental awareness, businesses are under pressure to adopt sustainable practices. AI-powered supply chain optimization can contribute to sustainablity goals by minimizing waste, reducing energy consumption and optimizing transportation routes. By streamlining operations and eliminating inefficiencies, businesses can lower their carbon footprint and contribute to a more environmentally friendly supply chain. Such practices not only align with corporate social responsibility initiatives but also resonate with environmentally conscious consumers.

Scalability and Adaptability

AI-powered supply chain optimization is highly scalable and adaptable to the changing needs of businesses. As companies grow and expand, their supply chain complexity also increases. AI algorithms can handle larger datasets, analyze more variables and accommodate the intricacies of a growing network. Furthermore, AI's ability to learn from new data means that algorithms become more refined and accurate over time, ensuring that optimization strategies evolve with changing market dynamics.

Improved Customer Satisfaction

Ultimately, the benefits of AI-powered supply chain optimization culminate in improved customer satisfaction, Businesses can deliver products to customers faster, with fewer errors and at competitive prices. By minimizing stockouts and ensuring on-time deliveries, customer loyalty and brand reputation are bolstered. Satisfied customers are more likely to become repeat buyers and recommend the brand to others, thus contributing to business growth and profitability.

Conclusion

The integration of AI-powered supply chain optimization into business operations heralds a new era of efficiency, cost savings and strategic decision making. By harnessing the power of AI to analyze real-time data, enhance demand forecasting, reduce operational costs and mitigate risks, businesses gain a competitive edge in a fast-paced global marketplace. The advantages extend to inventory management, supplier relationships, sustainability practices and scalability, all of which contribute to improved customer satisfaction and brand loyalty. As AI technology continues to evolve, businesses that embrace AI-powered supply chain optimization postion themselves for sustained growth, innovation and success in an ever-evolving business landscape.

Unleashing Creativity and Profit: The Power of Automated Content Creation

In an era driven by digital content consumption, the demand for engaging and relevant content has never been higher. As businesses, creators and individuals seek to maintain an online prescence, the concept of automated content creation has gained significant traction. Through the fusion of AI and technology, automated content creation offers an innovative and efficient way to generate a wide array of content, ranging from articles and social media posts to visuals and videos. Here I will explore the compelling reasons why automated content creation is a potent avenue for generating income. By harnessing AI-driven solutions, businesses and content creators can unlock new revenue streams, save time and stay competitive in the rapidly evolving digital landscape.

Efficiency and Time Savings

Automated content creation streamlines the content generation process, enabling businesses and creators to produce a larger volume of content in a shorter amount of time. Traditional content creation often involves hours of research, writing, editing and design work. With automation, content can be generated at a fraction of the time, allowing individuals to focus on higher level tasks such as strategy development and engagement with their audience. This newfound efficiency is especially valuable in fast paced industries where staying up-to-date and relevant is essential.

Diverse Content Creation

AI-powered content creation tools are not limited to a single format. From written articles and blog posts to social media captions, infographics and even video scripts, these tools offer a broad range of content generation capabilities. This diversity enables businesses and content creators to cater to various audience preferences across different platforms. By leveraging automated content creation, individuals can maintain a consistent online prescence and engage with audiences on multiple fronts, maximizing their reach and impact.

Scalability and Consistency

Scaling content creation efforts can be challenging, particularly for smaller businesses or solo content creators. Automated content creation offers a solution by enabling scalability without compromising quality or consistency. AI-driven tools can generate content with a cohesive tone, style and messaging, ensuring a seamless brand identity across all platforms. As content demands increase, automation allows for the rapid expansion of content production without straining resources or sacrificing quality.

Cost-Effectiveness

Traditional content creation often requires hiring multiple professionals, such as writers, designers and editors, which can be cost prohibitive for many businesses and individuals. Automated content creation significantly reduces labor costs, as businesses can achieve the same output with fewer human resources. This cost effectiveness makes content creation accessible to a wider range of businesses and creators, democratizing the playing field and enabling startups and entrepreneurs to compete with larger entities.

Customization and Personalization

While automation plays a central role in content creation, AI-driven tools are not devoid of personalization. Many automated content creation platforms allow for customization based on specific requirements, target audiences and branding guidelines. This level of customization ensures that generated content aligns with the desired messaging and resonates with the intended audience. Additionally, AI algorithms can analyze audience preferences and behaviours, enabling businesses to tailor content to individual preferences and enhance engagement.

Generating Niche and Evergreen Content

Niche markets often require specialized knowledge and expertise that not all content creators possess. Automated content creation allows businesses to generate niche-specific content efficiently, addressing the unique needs of their target audience. Furthermore, AI-powered tools can create evergreen content that remains relevant over time. This content not only provides value to the audience but also serves as a long term asset, driving consistent traffic and engagement, even after initial publication.

Data-Driven Insights

AI-powered content creation tools can provide valuable insights into content performance. By analyzing engagement metrics, click-through rates and audience behaviour, creators can gauge the effectiveness of their content strategies. These insights enable businesses and creators to refine their content approach, focusing on what resonates with their audience and adjusting their strategies accordingly. Data-driven decision making contributes to higher engagement, better content ROI and improved business outcomes.

Monetization Opportunities

Automated content creation opens the door to various monetization opportunities. Businesses and content creators can generate content at a faster pace, enabling them to offer premium content, subscriptions or exclusive access to their audience. Additionally, businesses can create content that aligns with affiliate marketing, sponsorships and advertising partnerships. As content output increases, the potential to collaborate with brands and capitalize on advertising revenue grows significantly.

Content Curation and Remixing

Automated content creation tools can also assist in content curation and remixing. These tools can analyze existing content, identify trends and generate new insights or perspectives. Businesses and creators can curate and remix content from various sources, adding value through commentary, analysis or repurposing. This approach not only saves time but also enables content creators to contribute to ongoing discussions and trends within their industry.

Challenges and Considerations

While automated content creation offers numerous benefits, it's important to recognize potential challenges. Content generated by AI may lack the nuances of human creativity and originality. Striking a balance between automation and human touch is crucial to maintain authenticity and uniqueness. Additionally, AI-generated content should be reviewed to ensure accuracy, relevance and alignment with brand values.

Conclusion

In the age of digital content consumption, automated content creation has emerged as a powerful tool that transforms the content creation landscape. Its efficiency, scalability, customization and monetization potential make it a compelling avenue for generating income. By harnessing AI-powered solutions, businesses and content creators can optimize their content strategies, engage their audiences and create new revenue streams. While challenges exist, the ability to strike a balance between automation and creativity ensures that the content remains authentic and resonates with the intended audience. As technology continues to advance, embracing automated content creation is not just a smart business move but a way to stay relevant and thrive in the ever evolving digital world.

Revolutionizing E-Commerce: The Profit Potential of AI-Driven Personalization

The e-commerce landscape has undergone a dramatic transformation with the advent of AI. Among its many applications, AI's impact on e-commerce personalization has been particularly significant. E-commerce personalization refers to tailoring shopping experiences to individual preferences and behaviours and AI plays a crucial role in making this customization scalable, efficient and effective. Let's look at the multifaceted ways in which AI-driven e-commerce personalization can generate revenue for businesses. By leveraging AI to enhance customer engagement, increase conversions and drive customer loyalty, businesses can unlock new avenues of growth in the competitive e-commerce market.

Enhanced Customer Experience

The cornerstone of AI-driven e-commerce personalization lies in providing an enhanced customer experience. AI algorithms analyze vast amounts of customer data, including browser behaviour, purchase history and demographic information, to create detailed customer profiles. Armed with this information, businesses can offer personalized recommendations, tailored product suggestions and curated content that resonates with individual preferences. By delivering a more relevant and engaging shopping experience, businesses can increase customer satisfaction and loyalty.

Increased Conversion Rates

AI-powered e-commerce personalization has a direct impact on conversion rates. When customers are presented with products that align with their interests and needs, they are more likely to make a purchase. AI algorithms predict customer preferences based on historical data, allowing businesses to showcase products that have a higher likelihood of conversion. Additionally, AI can optimize the placement and timing of personalized recommendations, maximizing their visibility and impact. As a result, businesses experience higher conversion rates, translating directly into increased revenue.

Targeted Marketing Campaigns

AI-driven e-commerce personalization extends beyond product recommendations; it also revolutionizes marketing campaigns, Businesses can segment their customer base into distinct groups based on demographics, behaviour and preferences. AI algorithms analyze these segments to create highly targeted marketing campaigns that resonate with each group. Personalized marketing messages, offers and incentives drive higher engagement and conversion rates, as customers feel understood and valued. By optimizing marketing efforts, businesses can generate more revenue while minimizing marketing costs.

Reduced Cart Abandonment

Cart abandonment is a significant challenge in e-commerce. AI-powered personalization helps address this issue by offering tailored incentives to encourage customers to complete their purchases. For instance, businesses can send personalized reminders or exclusive discounts to customers who abandoned their carts. AI algorithms can identify the optimal time and method to re-engage customers, increasing the likelihood of recovering potentially lost sales. By reducing cart abandonment rates, businesses can capture additional revenue that might have otherwise been left on the table.

Subscription and Membership Models

AI-driven e-commerce personalization enables businesses to explore subscription and membership models with greater success. By understanding customer preferences and purchasing patterns, AI algorithms can curate subscription boxes, membership benefits or loyalty programs that offer high value to customers. Businesses can incentivize customers to subscribe by tailoring these offerings to individual tastes, ensuring that customers receive products they genuinely desire. Subscriptions and memberships create recurring revenue streams while fostering long term customer relationships.

Cross-Selling and Upselling Opportunities

Cross-selling and upselling are proven strategies to increase average transaction values. AI-powered e-commerce personalization takes these strategies to the next level. By analyzing customer behaviours and purchase history, AI algorithms identify complementary products or higher tier options that align with customer preferences. During the shopping journey, businesses can present these suggestions seamlessly, enhancing the value proposition for customers. This personalized approach not only increases transaction values but also enhances customer satisfaction by providing valuable recommendations.

Dynamic Pricing Optimization

AI-driven e-commerce personalization also extends to dynamic pricing optimization. AI algorithms can analyze market trends, competitor pricing and customer behaviour to adjust prices in real time. Businesses can offer personalized discounts, promotions or pricing tiers based on customer loyalty, browsing history or purchase frequency. This approach creates a sense of exclusivity and incentivizes customers to make purchases while maximizing revenue through dynamic pricing strategies.

Retargeting and Remarketing

Retargeting and remarketing are essential tactics to bring back potential customers who have interacted with a business but haven't made a purchase. AI-driven e-commerce personalization amplifies the effectiveness of these strategies. By analyzing customer behaviours and preferences, businesses can create highly relevant retargeting campaigns that resonate with individual interests. AI algorithms identify the most opportune moments to retarget customers with tailored messages, ensuring that they receive compelling incentives to return and convert.

Customer Lifetime Value Enhancement

AI-driven e-commerce personalization has a profound impact on customer lifetime value (CLV). Businesses that provide personalized experiences and relevant recommendations foster strong customer relationships, resulting in repeat purchases and long term loyalty. Higher CLV translates to a steady stream of revenue from existing customers, reducing the need for costly customer acquisition efforts. By investing in AI-powered personalization, businesses can nurture valuable customer relationships that yield consistent and sustainable revenue over time.

Conclusion

In the dynamic realm of e-commerce, AI-driven personalization has emerged as a catalyst for revenue generation and business growth. By leveraging AI-algorithms to enhance customer experiences, increase conversion rates and drive customer loyalty, businesses can create a competitive advantage in the crowded e-commerce landscape. The benefits extend beyond immediate revenue gains; businesses also foster lasting customer relationships, reduce cart abandonment rates and optimize marketing campaigns. As AI technology continues to evolve, the potential for revenue generation through e-commerce personalization is boundless. Embracing AI-driven personalization is not just a smart business strategy; it's a transformative approach that propels businesses toward success in the digital age.

Transforming Real Estate Market Analysis: The Profit Potential of AI-Driven Platforms

The real estate market is a complex and dynamic industry, with investors, developers and individuals seeking accurate and timely insights to make informed decisions. With the advent of AI, the traditional landscape of real estate market analysis is undergoing a profound transformation. AI-driven platforms are revolutionizing how data is collected, processed and analyzed, offering advanced predictive capabilities and unparalleled accuracy. I will explain here how AI-driven platforms have the potential to turn real estate market analysis into a profitable venture. By harnessing the power of AI to provide actionable insights, risk assessment and investment opportunities, businesses can unlock new revenue streams and thrive in the ever evolving real estate sector.

Enhanced Data Analytics

AI-driven platforms excel in handling massive volumes of data, making them invaluable tools for real estate market analysis. Traditional methods of data collection often suffer from limitations in scale, accuracy and speed. AI, on the other hand, can process vast datasets, including property prices, historical sales data, markets trends and socioeconomic indicators. with exceptional efficiency. This level of data analytics empowers businesses to make data-driven decisions based on real-time insights, improving the accuracy of market forecasts and investment strategies.

Predictive Market Trends

AI-driven platforms go beyond static data analysis; they offer predictive capabilities that transform real estate market analysis into a forward looking endeavor. By analyzing historical data and identifying patterns, AI algorithms can predict future market trends, property values and demand shifts. Investors and businesses can leverage these predictions to seize opportunities, mitigate risks and position themselves ahead of market fluctuations. Predictive insights enable proactive decision making, leading to more favorable investment outcomes and increased profitability.

Risk Assessment and Mitigation

Real estate investments are inherently risky and the ability to assess and mitigate risks is crucial for success. AI-driven platforms excel in risk assessment by analyzing a multitude of variables that impact property values and market dynamics. From economic indicators and interest rates to neighborhood crime rates and infrastructure developments, AI algorithms can calculate risk scores and provide insights into potential challenges. Businesses can make more informed decisions by factoring in these risk assessments, reducing the likelihood of losses and enhancing their financial stability.

Investment Opportunity Identification

AI-driven platforms have the potential to uncover hidden investment opportunities that might go unnoticed through traditional methods. By processing diverse datasets and recognizing emerging trends, AI algorithms can identify neighborhoods or property types with growth potential. Businesses can target undervalued properties or areas on the brink of revitalization, capitalizing on early stage opportunities. This ability to identify lucrative investments before they become mainstream contributes to generating substantial returns on investment.

Personalized Investment Strategies

AI-driven platforms offer personalized investment strategies tailored to individual preferences and goals. By analyzing investor profiles, risk tolerance and financial objectives, AI algorithms can recommend investment options that align with each investor's unique circumstances. Personalized strategies enhance investor engagement, foster trust and create a sense of value added service. This level of customization sets AI-driven platforms apart, driving investor loyalty and repeat business.

Market Transparency and Data Visualization

AI-driven platforms enhance market transparency by presenting data in accessible and visual formats. Complex market trends, property comparisons and investment analyses can be presented through intuitive data visualizations. This clarity enables investors and businesses to understand the market dynamics more comprehensively, allowing for more strategic decisions. Additionally, data visualization simplifies the communication of investment opportunities to potential investors, creating a compelling presentation that showcases the potential profitability of a property or project.

Automated Valuation Models (AVMs)

Automated Valuation Models (AVMs) powered by AI are transforming property valuation processes. AVMs leverage AI algorithms to assess property values by analyzing a wide range of factors, including property attributes, market trends and recent sales data. AVMs provide faster and more accurate property valuations compared to traditional methods, benefiting investors, lenders and real estate professionals. Businesses can offer AVM services through AI-driven platforms, generating revenue from property valuation requests and subscriptions.

Informed Investment Strategies

AI-driven platforms empower businesses to develop informed investment strategies that cater to changing market conditions. By continuously analyzing data and adjusting investment recommendations, these platforms provide real-time insights into optimal investment strategies. Investors can capitalize on short term opportunities while also adhering to long term goals. Businesses that offer AI-driven investment strategies can attract a wider investor base, offering a compelling value proposition that combines cutting-edge technology with financial expertise.

Real-Time Market Updates

The real estate market is influenced by a myriad of factors, from economic indicators to regulatory changes. AI-driven platforms provide real-time updates on market conditions, helping businesses and investors stay ahead of the curve. Businesses can monetize this real-time information by offering subscription based access to exclusive market updates and insights. This subscription model provides a steady revenue stream while positioning the platform as a trusted source of timely and valuable information.

Conclusion

AI-driven platforms are reshaping the landscape of real estate market analysis, offering insights, predictions and opportunities that were previously unimaginable. By exploiting the power of AI to enhance data analytics, predict market trends, assess risks and personalize investment strategies, businesses can turn real estate market analysis into a lucrative venture. The benefits extend beyond immediate revenue gains; AI-driven platforms enhance investor engagement, foster market transparency and position businesses as leaders in the evolving real estate sector. As AI technology continues to evolve, the potential for profit from AI-driven real estate market analysis is limitless. Embracing AI-driven platforms is not just a savvy business move; it's a transformational approach that positions businesses to thrive in the dynamic world of real estate.

Empowering Sustainability: AI's Role in Energy Efficiency for Cost Savings and Environmental Impact

The global pursuit of sustainable living and environmental preservation has spurred a significant shift toward energy efficiency. In this endeavor, AI has emerged as a powerful ally, transforming the way we manage energy consumption, AI's capabilities in data analysis, pattern recognition and automation enable the creation of energy efficiency systems that not only save money for consumers but also yield positive environmental impacts. Let's explore the multifaceted ways in which AI-driven energy efficiency systems contribute to cost savings and environmental sustainability, fostering a harmonious relationship between economic prosperity and ecological preservation.

Data-Driven Insights for Consumption Patterns

AI-driven energy efficiency systems rely on sophisticated algorithms to analyze vast amounts of data related to energy consumption. By processing historical consumption patterns, weather data, occupancy rates and equipment efficiency, AI can identify trends and anomalies that manual analysis might overlook. This comprehensive understanding of consumption patterns allows consumers and businesses to optimize energy usage by adjusting their behaviour and operations. By providing real-time insights, AI-driven systems empower users to make informed decisions that result in reduced energy consumption and cost savings.

Automated Demand Response

AI-enabled energy efficiency systems offer automated demand response mechanisms. These systems can predict peak demand periods based on historical data and current conditions. By automatically adjusting energy intensive operations during peak demand times, such as adjusting HVAC settings or temporarily reducing non-essential equipment loads, AI-driven systems help balance supply and demand on the grid. This not only leads to cost savings for consumers through lower peak demand charges but also alleviates strain on the energy grid, enhancing overall reliability and minimizing need for additional infrastructure.

Smart Building Management

AI-driven energy efficiency extends to smart building management systems. These systems utilize sensors and IoT (Internet of Things) devices to collect real-time data on occupancy, temperature, lighting and equipment usage. AI algorithms analyze this data to optimize building operations, adjusting heating, cooling and lighting based on actual occupancy and usage patterns. The result is a significant reduction in energy waste and increased cost savings as buildings operate in alignment with real-time conditions rather than fixed schedules.

Predictive Maintenance

Energy efficiency systems powered by AI can also improve equipment maintenance practices. By continuously monitoring the performance of equipment, AI algorithms can detect early signs of wear and potential malfunctions. Predictive maintenance ensures that equipment is serviced and repaired before major breakdowns occur, preventing costly emergency repairs and downtime. Efficient equipment operation translates to reduced energy consumption and extended equipment lifetimes, resulting in both financial savings and a reduced environmental footprint.

Optimized Energy Consumption

AI-driven energy efficiency systems optimize energy consumption across various sectors, from residential to commercial and industrial. These systems consider factors such as occupancy, temperature, humidity and lighting preferences to adjust energy usage in real time. By aligning consumption with actual needs, businesses and consumers avoid wasteful practices, ultimately saving money on energy bills. Moreover, this reduction in energy demand contributes to a decreased reliance on fossil fuels, mitigating greenhouse gas emissions and promoting environmental preservation.

Renewable Energy Integration

AI's ability to process and analyze data is essential for integrating renewable energy sources into the energy grid. Renewables, such as solar and wind power are intermittent by nature, making their integration complex. AI-driven energy management systems predict the availability of renewable energy based on weather forecasts and historical patterns. By optimizing energy usage in response to renewables' availability, businesses and consumers can maximize the utilization of clean energy, reducing dependence on non-renewable sources and minimizing environmental impact.

Carbon Footprint Reduction

One of the most profound impacts of AI-driven energy efficiency systems is their contribution to reducing carbon footprints. AI algorithms analyze energy consumption and identify areas of inefficiency. By suggesting energy saving actions, optimizing equipment performance and automating demand response, AI-driven systems facilitate substantial reductions in energy use. This translates to fewer greenhouse gas emissions, aligning with global efforts to combat climate change and create a more sustainable future.

Incentivizing Behaviour Change

AI-driven energy efficiency systems can incentivize positive behaviour change among consumers and businesses. Real-time feedback on energy consumption, personalized tips for energy savings and comparisons with similar households or businesses can motivate users to adopt more energy efficient practices. By gamifying energy conservation and offering rewards for achieving energy reduction goals, AI-driven systems create a sense of accomplishment and engagement, ultimately resulting in sustained energy savings and cost reductions.

Policy Compliance and Reporting

AI-driven energy efficiency systems facilitate compliance with energy efficiency regulations and reporting requirements. Businesses and institutions can use these systems to monitor and report energy consumption, assuring adherence to energy efficiency standards set by regulatory authorities. Accurate reporting not only avoids penalties but also positions businesses as responsible stewards of the environment, enhancing their reputation and credibility.

Conclusion

As societies around the world strive for a sustainable future, AI-driven energy efficiency systems emerge as transformative tools that bridge the gap between economic prosperity and environmental stewardship. By harnessing AI's data analysis, predictive capabilities and automation, businesses and consumers can make smarter energy decisions that result in cost savings and a positive impact on the environment. These systems optimize energy consumption, integrate renewable sources and incentivize behaviour change, fostering a culture of sustainablility. The synergy between AI and energy efficiency exemplifies how technological innovation can harmonize economic growth with ecological preservation, ultimately shaping a brighter, more sustainable future for generations to come.

Unleashing Global Opportunities: The Financial Triumph of Advanced AI Language Translation Tools

In a rapidly globalizing world, effective communication across languages has become a paramount requirement for businesses and individuals alike. The emergence of advanced AI language translation tools has revolutionized the way we bridge linguistic barriers. These tools, powered by sophisticated algorithms and deep learning, offer unparalleled accuracy and efficiency in translating text and speech. In this chapter I will delve into the myriad ways in which advanced AI language translation tools can be a financial winner. By facilitating international expansion, enhancing cross-cultural collaboration and unlocking new markets, these tools have the potential to transform businesses and generate substantial revenue.

Global Market Expansion

Advanced AI language translation tools pave the way for businesses to expand their reach into global markets. In the past, language barriers often hindered the penetration of foreign markets, requiring significant investments in translation services and human resources. However, AI-driven translation tools offer a cost effective and scalable solution. Businesses can effortlessly translate websites, marketing materials, product descriptions and customer communications, ensuring that their offerings are accessible and comprehensible to diverse audiences worldwide. By breaking down language barriers, businesses can tap into new customer bases, increasing sales and revenue streams.

Enhanced Cross-Cultural Collaboration

Effective communication is essential for collaboration across international teams and AI language translation tools play a pivotal role in facilitating this collaboration. Businesses with global operations can utilize these tools to bridge communication gaps between teams speaking different languages. Meetings, emails and documents can be seamlessly translated, ensuring that all team members can actively contribute and understand discussions. Enhanced cross-cultural collaboration leads to improved productivity, faster decision making and the successful execution of projects, ultimately contributing to cost savings and revenue growth.

Accelerated Content Localization

Localization is a critical aspect of global marketing and content distribution. Advanced AI language translation tools expedite the content localization process by automatically adapting content to suit cultural nuances and linguistic preferences. This enables businesses to swiftly launch localized campaigns, product releases and marketing materials, reducing time to market and seizing time sensitive opportunities. Accelerated content localization not only generates revenue from new markets but also enhances brand reputation by showcasing a commitment to delivering tailored and culturally relevant content.

Customized Customer Engagement

Effective customer engagement is the cornerstone of successful businesses and AI language translation tools play a pivotal role in enhancing this engagement on a global scale. Businesses can use AI-driven translation to interact with customers in their native languages across various channels, such as websites, social media and customer support. This personalized approach establishes a stronger rapport with customers, leading to higher levels of trust, loyalty and repeat business, Satisfied and engaged customers are more likely to make purchases, advocate for the brand and contribute to revenue growth.

Unlocking New Market Opportunities

AI language translation tools open doors to previously untapped markets. Businesses can identify emerging markets with high demand for their products or services and leverage these tools to quickly adapt their offerings to the local language. This agility allows businesses to capitalize on new market opportunities before competitors, securing a strong foothold and generating substantial revenue. The ability to swiftly enter diverse markets while maintaining language relevance can be a game changer for businesses looking to diversify and expand revenue streams.

Optimized E-Commerce and Global Sales

E-commerce has transcended geographical boundaries, making AI language translation tools invaluable for global online businesses. By offering seamless translation of product descriptions, reviews and checkout processes, these tools create a frictionless shopping experience for customers around the world. Customers are more likely to make purchases when they can understand product information and navigate the buying process in their preferred language. Optimizing e-commerce platforms for global sales drives higher conversion rates, resulting in increased revenue for businesses.

Efficient Communication in Multilingual Supply Chains

Supply chains often span multiple countries, cultures and languages. Advanced AI language translation tools streamline communication within multilingual supply chains, reducing miscommunication, delays and errors. Accurate translation of orders, invoices and logistics information ensures that suppliers, manufacturers and distributors can collaborate seamlessly across linguistic barriers. Efficient supply chain communication translates to cost savings, faster operations and optimized resource allocation, ultimately contributing to increased profitability.

Improved Regulatory Compliance and Documentation

Businesses operating in multiple countries must navigate varying regulatory requirements and compliance standards. Advanced AI language translation tools aid in the translation of legal documents, contracts and compliance related communications. This accuracy ensures that businesses remain compliant with regulations and avoid legal disputes that could result in financial penalties. Smooth compliance processes and accurate documentation safeguard a business's financial health and reputation while minimizing legal expenses.

Translation as a Service (TaaS) Revenue Model

The emergence of advanced AI language translation tools has given rise to a new revenue model known as Translation as a Service (TaaS). Businesses can offer translation services to other businesses, individuals or institutions on a subscription or per-use basis. AI-powered TaaS platforms can generate revenue from both domestic and international clients, offering a consistent income stream. The scalability and automation offered by AI-driven tools make TaaS an attractive business model, providing financial returns with relatively low operational overhead.

Conclusion

The financial success of advanced AI-language translation tools is evident in their ability to transcend linguistic barriers and transform businesses on a global scale. From facilitating international expansion and cross cultural collaboration to unlocking new market opportunities and optimizing customer engagement, these tools offer a myriad of benefits that translate directly into revenue growth. The intersection of AI and language translation technology exemplifies how technological innovation can drive economic prosperity while fostering cross cultural understanding. As AI continues to advance, the financial potential of these tools will only grow, making them an indispensable asset for businesses seeking to thrive in the interconnected world of the 21st century.

Safeguarding Prosperity: The Financial Triumph of AI-Driven Cybersecurity Solutions for Businesses

In an era defined by digital connectivity and technological advancements, the significance of cybersecurity cannot be overstated. The increasing sophistication of cyber threats has prompted businesses to seek robust solutions to safeguard their digital assets and sensitive information. Enter AI-driven cybersecurity solutions, which have emerged as indispensable tools in the battle against cyber attacks. In this chapter I will examine how AI-driven cybersecurity solutions offer financial benefits to businesses by thwarting cyber threats, preventing data breaches, reducing operational costs and preserving brand reputation. By embracing AI-driven cybersecurity, businesses can fortify their defenses and navigate the digital landscape with confidence.

Enhanced Threat Detection and Prevention

The threat landscape in the digital realm is ever evolving, with cyber criminals devising new techniques to breach security measures. AI-driven cybersecurity solutions utilize machine learning algorithms to analyze massive volumes of data and identify patterns indicative of cyber threats. These solutions can detect anomalies and potential breaches that might elude traditional security systems. By identifying threats at an early stage, businesses can prevent costly data breaches, minimize the impact of attacks and avoid financial losses associated with data theft, downtime and reputational damage.

Compliance and Regulatory Savings

Various industries are subject to stringent regulatory requirements regarding data protection and cybersecurity. Non.compliance can result in hefty fines and legal consequences. AI-driven cybersecurity solutions help businesses achieve and maintain compliance by identifying vulnerabilities and potential breaches. By consistently adhering to regulatory standards, businesses avoid costly penalties and legal actions, safeguarding their financial health.

Reducing Operational Costs

Traditional cybersecurity approaches often involve manual monitoring and response, which can be resource-intensive. AI-driven solutions automate many aspects of cybersecurity operations, significantly reducing the workload on human security teams. These systems can analyze vast amounts of data in real time, identifying threats and anomalies far more efficiently than manual processes. By optimizing cybersecurity operations and minimizing the need for human intervention, businesses can reduce operational costs while enhancing security measures.

Minimizing Downtime and Operational Disruptions

Cyberattacks can lead to substantial downtime, disrupting business operations and resulting in lost productivity and revenue. AI-driven cybersecurity solutions are designed to protect threads early and respond swiftly. By mitigating cyber threats before they escalate, these systems minimize operational disruptions and downtime. Businesses can maintain business continuity, meet customer demands and avoid the financial losses associated with extended downtime.

Enhanced Threat Detection and Response

Traditional cybersecurity solutions often struggle to keep up with the speed and complexity of modern cyber threats. AI-driven solutions excel in threat detection and response by leveraging machine learning algorithms. These systems can analyze vast datasets and identify patterns indicative of cyber threats.. They can also respond to threats in real time, automatically isolating affected systems and mitigating risks. Enhanced threat detection and response capabilities ensure that businesses can prevent cyberattacks from causing financial harm.

Reduced False Positives

Traditional cybersecurity systems can generate numerous false positive alerts, overwhelming security teams and diverting resources away from genuine threats. AI-driven solutions are designed to learn from historical data and adapt over time, reducing false positives. By improving the accuracy of threat detection, these systems enable security teams to focus their efforts on genuine threats, optimizing resource allocation and reducing the financial burden associated with false alarms.

Preserving Brand Reputation

A cybersecurity breach can have long-lasting effects on a business's brand reputation. Customers, partners and stakeholders can lose trust in a company that fails to protect their data. The financial consequences of a damaged brand reputation can be significant, including decreased customer loyalty, lost business opportunities and decreased market share. AI-driven cybersecurity solutions help businesses preserve their brand reputation by proactively protecting against cyber threats. This, in turn, maintains customer trust and loyalty, ultimately contributing to financial success.

Preventing Intellectual Property Theft

For many businesses, intellectual property (IP) represents a significant financial asset. Cyberattacks aimed at stealing IP can result in substantial financial losses and the erosion of competitive advantages. AI-driven cybersecurity solutions are equipped to protect against IP theft by identifying and thwarting attempts to breach sensitive data repositories. The prevention of IP theft ensures that businesses can maintain their market position and protect their financial interests.

Scalability and Resource Efficiency

AI-driven cybersecurity solutions are highly scalable, making them adaptable to the evolving needs of businesses. As businesses grow and their digital footprint expands, these solutions can scale alongside them without significant increases in costs. The resource efficiency offered by AI-driven solutions ensures that businesses can maintain robust cybersecurity measures while optimizing costs and resource allocation.

Conclusion

AI-driven cybersecurity solutions have emerged as powerful allies in the ongoing battle against cyber threats. The financial benefits they offer are substantial, ranging from preventing data breaches and reducing operational costs to preserving brand reputation and ensuring regulatory compliance. By embracing AI-driven cybersecurity, businesses can fortify their defenses, mitigate financial risks and achieve operational continuity. As the digital landscape continues to evolve, the financial triumph of AI-driven cybersecurity solutions becomes increasingly evident. For businesses committed to safeguarding their prosperity, these solutions are not just a necessity; they are a strategic imperative.

Transforming Operations: The Strategic Value of AI-Driven Predictive Maintenance for Industrial Equipment

The industrial landscape is characterized by complex machinery and equipment that drive production, manufacturing and critical processes. The maintenance of these assets is crucial for ensuring operational efficiency, minimizing downtime and maximizing productivity. In recent years, the integration of AI has revolutionized maintenance strategies, particularly with the advent of predictive maintenance. Here I will delve into the many ways in which AI-driven predictive maintenance for industrial equipment offers significant benefits for businesses. By preventing unplanned downtime, optimizing maintenance schedules, reducing operational costs and enhancing asset performance, AI-built systems are proving to be indispensable tools for boosting operational efficiency and achieving substantial financial gains.

Preventing Unplanned Downtime

Unplanned equipment failures can bring industrial operations to a halt, resulting in lost production time, revenue and customer satisfaction. AI-driven predictive maintenance uses real-time data and machine learning algorithms to monitor the health of industrial equipment. By analyzing factors such as equipment performance,sensor readings and historical data, these systems can identify early signs of impending failures. This proactive approach allows businesses to intervene before a critical failure occurs, preventing unplanned downtime and its associated financial losses.

Optimizing Maintenance Schedules

Traditional maintenance strategies often rely on routine schedules, leading to either unnecessary preventive maintenance or instances of neglect. AI-driven predictive maintenance transforms this paradigm by tailoring maintenance schedules to the actual condition of equipment. By assessing the real-time health of industrial assets, AI-built systems can predict when maintenance is needed, based on wear and tear, usage patterns and degradation trends. This optimization minimizes both the frequency of maintenance and the risk of equipment failure, resulting in cost savings and improved resource allocation.

Reducing Operational Costs

AI-driven predictive maintenance minimizes operational costs by targeting maintenance efforts precisely where they are needed. Unplanned downtime can result in significant revenue losses due to halted production and reduced efficiency. Predictive maintenance prevents such disruptions by addressing issues before they escalate, reducing the need for costly emergency repairs and unscheduled maintenance activities. Moreover, by optimizing maintenance schedules and avoiding unnecessary work, businesses can allocate resources more efficiently and minimize labor, material and overhead costs.

Enhancing Asset Performance and Lifespan

Industrial equipment is a substantial investment and maximizing the performance and lifespan of these assets is crucial for achieving a strong return on investment. AI-driven predictive maintenance systems continually monitor equipment performance and usage patterns. By identifying and addressing issues early, businesses can extend the operational life of equipment and ensure that it performs at its optimal capacity. Enhanced asset performance not only increases productivity but also delays the need for expensive replacements, resulting in long term financial gains.

Data-Driven Decision Making

AI-driven predictive maintenance relies on data analytics to make informed decisions about maintenance activities. This data-driven approach ensures that maintenance decisions are based on accurate and objective information rather than subjective assessments. Businesses can track key performance indicators, equipment health metrics and maintenance history to develop a comprehensive understanding of their assets. Data-driven decision making reduces the risk of over-maintenance or under-maintenance, enhancing maintenance effectiveness and generating cost savings.

Improved Inventory Management

Predictive maintenance systems enable businesses to manage spare parts and inventory more effectively. By accurately predicting when specific components are likely to fail, these systems allow for precise inventory management. Businesses can stock the necessary spare parts and materials in advance, reducing downtime associated with waiting for replacement parts to arrive. Improved inventory management leads to faster repairs, shorter equipment downtimes and streamlined maintenance operations, ultimately resulting in financial savings.

Labor Efficiency and Resource Allocation

AI-driven predictive maintenance optimizes labor efficiency by ensuring that maintenance teams are deployed where they are most needed. Maintenance tasks can be planned in advance, based on predictive insights, allowing for efficient allocation of resources and personnel. This approach minimizes the time spent on routine inspections and reduces the need for reactive maintenance activities. Labor efficiency contributes to cost savings and enhances the productivity of maintenance teams.

Competitive Edge and Customer Satisfaction

Businesses that implement AI-driven predictive maintenance gain a competitive edge in their industry. Reliable equipment performance and minimal downtime translate to consistent production output, higher product quality and improved customer satisfaction. Customers value suppliers that can deliver products on time, without disruptions and predictive maintenance enables businesses to meet these expectations. Positive customer experiences lead to repeat business, positive reviews and referrals, all of which contribute to revenue growth.

Conclusion

AI-driven predictive maintenance is a game changer for businesses operating in the industrial sector. By leveraging real-time data, machine learning algorithms and predictive insights, businesses can prevent unplanned downtime, optimize maintenance schedules, reduce operational costs and enhance asset performance. The financial benefits are undeniable – cost savings from reduced downtime, efficient resource allocation and optimized inventory management are just a few of the advantages that contribute to improved profitablitity. As AI technology continues to evolve, the potential for even greater financial gains from predictive maintenance becomes increasingly apparent. By embracing AI-built systems for predictive maintenance, businesses can not only enhance their operational efficiency but also secure their competitive position in the ever evolving industrial landscape.

Maximizing Investor Returns: Harnessing AI for Private Investors

The world of investing is ever evolving and as technology continues to reshape various industries, AI has emerged as a powerful tool for private investors seeking to make substantial gains. AI's ability to process vast amounts of data, identify patterns and predict market trends has the potential to revolutionize the investment landscape. Here I will explore how AI can empower private investors to make informed decisions, optimize their portfolios and ultimately increase their wealth.

Data-Driven Decision Making

One of the most significant advantages of AI in investing is its capacity to process and analyze large volumes of data quickly and accurately. Traditional investment strategies often rely on human analysis, which can be limited by cognitive biases and information overload. AI, on the other hand, excels in handling diverse data sources, including financial reports, news sentiment, social media trends and economic indicators. This allows private investors to base their decisions on a comprehensive understanding of the market landscape, minimizing the risk of overlooking crucial information.

Machine learning algorithms can identify hidden patterns and correlations that might be imperceptible to human investors. By analyzing historical data, AI can uncover trends and relationships that inform predictions about future market movements. Private investors armed with AI-generated insights can identify opportunities and make well informed investment choices that have the potential to yield substantial profits.

Predictive Analytics

AI's predictive capabilities have the potential to give private investors a comprehensive edge in the market. Machine learning algorithms can forecast market trends, asset price movements and even potential disruptions. Through analyzing historical data and real-time information, AI can generate predictive models that assist investors in making decisions that align with their risk tolerance and investment goals. Furthermore AI-powered algorithms can continuously learn and adapt, based on market changes. This adaptability allows them to refine their predictions over time, increasing their accuracy and reliability. By utilizing AI-generated forecasts, private investors can strategically position themselves in markets that are poised for growth, thus increasing their chances of generating substantial returns.

Risk Management

Investing inherently involves risk, but AI can play a crucial role in managing and mitigating these risks. Machine learning algorithms can assess the risk associated with different investment options by considering historical volatility, market sentiment and macroeconomic factors. AI can generate risk profiles for various assets, helping private investors make informed decisions that align with their risk appetite. Moreover, AI's real-time monitoring capabilities enable investors to react swiftly to sudden market changes. By analyzing news sentiment and other relevant data, AI can provide timely alerts, allowing investors to adjust their portfolios in response to unforeseen events. This proactive risk management approach can help prevent significant losses and preserve capital.

Portfolio Opimization

AI's computational power extends to portfolio optimization, where it can assist private investors in constructing portfolios that maximize returns while minimizing risk. Traditional portfolio management often relies on diversification strategies, but AI can take this approach to a new level. By analyzing correlations between different assets and considering complex factors, AI can recommend optimal asset allocations tailored to an investor's unique circumstances. Furthermore, AI can adapt portfolio recommendations in real-time as market conditions change. This dynamic optimization ensures that the portfolio remains aligned with the investor's goals and the evolving market landscape. By relying on AI to fine-tune their portfolios, private investors can enhance their potential for generating substantial profits.

Conclusion

Artificial Intelligence is not a guaranteed path to riches but its potential to revolutionize the investment landscape is undeniable. Private investors who harness AI's capabilities can benefit from data-driven decision making, predictive analytics, advanced risk management and portfolio optimization. However, it's crucial to acknowledge that AI is not a replacement for human judgement; rather, it is a powerful tool that complements and enhances investors' abilities. As AI continues to advance, its applications in the investment realm will likely become even more sophisticated. Private investors who embrace this technology and integrate it into their strategies can position themselves at the forefront of an evolving and competitive market. While challenges and uncertainties remain, the integration of AI in investment practices has the potential to yield substantial returns, ultimately contributing to the financial success of private investors.

Navigating Climate Breakdown: Harnessing AI for Sustainable Profitability

The escalating climate breakdown poses significant challenges to various aspects of society, including economics and investments. However, in the face of these challenges, AI has emerged as a powerful ally for individuals and businesses seeking to not only mitigate the impacts of climate change but also capitalize on sustainable opportunities. I will explore here the ways in which AI can empower individuals to make informed decisions that generate profits while contributing to environmental sustainability.

Sustainable Investment Strategies

Climate breakdown has prompted a shift towards sustainable investing, where environmental, social and governance (ESG) considerations play a central role in decision making. AI can assist investors in identifying companies that align with these values. Machine learning algorithms can analyze vast amounts of data from financial reports, news sources and social media to assess a company's ESG performance. By quantifying ESG metrics, AI enables investors to make data-driven decisions that reflect their ethical and sustainable preferences. Furthermore, AI can evaluate a company's resilience to climate related risks. With the increasing frequency of extreme weather events, companies that can adapt and thrive in a changing climate are likely to outperform their peers. AI-powered risk assessments can assist investors in identifying businesses that are better prepared to weather the challenges posed by climate breakdown, leading to more profitable investment choices.

Renewable Energy Investments

The transition to renewable energy sources is a critical aspect of addressing climate breakdown. AI can play a pivotal role in optimizing the profitability of renewable energy investments. For instance, AI-powered predictive analytics can forecast energy demand patterns and fluctuations, enabling investors to make informed decisions about when to buy and sell energy stocks. Moreover, AI can analyze data from various sources to identify promising renewable energy projects, such as solar farms and wind turbines, based on factors like location, weather patterns and energy infrastructure.

In the realm of energy storage, AI can optimize battery usage and charging strategies, enhancing the efficiency and profitability of energy storage systems. This is particularly relevant as intermittent renewable sources like solar and wind require efficient storage solutions to ensure a consistent energy supply.

Climate-Resilient Agriculture

Agriculture is highly sensitive to climate conditions, making it susceptible to the effects of climate breakdown. AI can help investors capitalize on opportunities within the agricultural sector by predicting climate related challenges and optimizing agricultural practices. For example, AI can analyze weather data, soil conditions and crop health to provide insights that assist investors in identifying potential areas for agricultural investment. Precision agriculture, driven by AI, can increase crop yields while reducing resource consumption. AI-powered sensors and drones can monitor crops in real-time, identifying areas that require irrigation, fertilization or pest control. This data driven approach not only improves agricultural productivity but also promotes sustainability by minimizing resource waste.

Climate-Responsible Real Estate

The real estate sector is not immune to the impacts of climate breakdown, with rising sea levels and extreme weather events affecting property values and investment decisions. AI can aid investors in making climate-resilient real estate investments. Through analyzing geographic and climate data, AI can identify regions that are less prone to climate risks, helping investors make informed choices about where to invest in properties. Moreover, AI can assess the energy efficiency of buildings. Buildings are responsible for a significant portion of global energy consumption and energy efficient stuctures are not only environmentally responsible but also financially beneficial. AI-driven analyses can identify properties with the potential for energy savings through improvements in insulation, heating, cooling and lighting systems.

Green Innovation and Startups

The urgency of addressing climate breakdown has spurred innovation in green technologies and solutions. AI can help investors identify promising startups that are developing groundbreaking solutions for sustainability challenges. Natural language processing algorithms can analyze startup pitches, business plans and industry trends to identify startups with the potential for disruptive impact.

Venture capitalists and angel investors can benefit from AI-driven insights that assess the viability and scalability of green startups. By supporting innovative ventures that address climate related issues, investors not only contribute to global sustainability efforts but also position themselves to profit from the growth of these emerging industries.

Conclusion

The worsening climate breakdown presents a complex challenge that requires comprehensive and innovative solutions. AI, with its ability to process vast amounts of data and generate valuable insights, has the potential to revolutionize how we approach this challenge from an investment perspective. By aligning financial goals with environmental sustainability, individuals and businesses can capitalize on profitable opportunities while actively contributing to a more resilient and sustainable future.

It is important to note that AI is not a standalone solution but a tool that works best in collaboration with human expertise and ethical considerations. While AI offers significant potential for profit in the face of climate breakdown, investors must remain vigilant in evaluating both the financial and ethical implications of their decisions. By utilizing the power of AI to drive sustainable profitability, we can pave the way for a more prosperous and resilient future for generations to come.

Leveraging AI for Increased Efficiency and Productivity: Working Smart to Earn More with Less Effort

In today's fast-paced world, the pusuit of striking a balance between work and personal life is more relevant than ever. The advent of AI has opened up new avenues for individuals to achieve greater efficiency, productivity and financial success while simultaneously reducing their workload. Let's examine how AI technologies can be employed to work smarter, enabling individuals to earn more while investing less time and effort.

Automating Routine Tasks

AI-driven information is a game-changer when it comes to reducing the time and effort spent on routine tasks. Many professionals are bogged down by repetitive and time-consuming activities that can be easily handled by AI-powered systems. For instance, in the realm of business and finance, AI can streamline data entry, report generation and basic customer interactions, freeing up individuals to focus on higher value tasks that require human creativity and critical thinking. By delegating routine tasks to AI, individuals can significantly reduce their workload, allowing them to channel their energy into strategic decision making and innovation. This shift in focus can lead to higher quality outcomes and ultimately, increased earnings.

Personalized Time Management

AI-driven personal assistents and scheduling tools can optimize time management by analyzing work patterns, priorities and deadlines. These tools can generate customized schedules that maximize productivity by allocating time to tasks when individuals are most focused and energetic. By optimizing work schedules, individuals can maintain high levels of productivity without feeling overwhelmed. Furthermore, AI can help individuals identify time wasting habits and suggest improvements. Analyzing digital behaviours, AI can provide insights into time allocation, screen time and multitasking tendencies. Armed with this information, individuals can make informed decisions to work more efficiently and dedicate time to activities that truly matter, both professionally and personally.

Enhanced Decision Support

Making informed decisions is crucial for success, but the information overload that often accompanies modern work can be overwhelming. AI-powered decision support systems can sift through vast amounts of data to extract relevant insights and present them in a comprehensive format. For investors and business professionals, AI can provide real-time market analysis, identify trends and predict potential opportunities. By relying on AI-generated insights, individuals can make well-informed decisions quickly, reducing the time spent on research and analysis. This not only leads to better outcomes but also allows individuals to optimize their earning potential with minimal effort.

Personalized Learning and Skill Development

Continuous learning and skill development are essential for career growth and earning potential. AI-driven platforms can provide personalized learning paths based on individual strengths, weaknesses and career goals. These platforms can analyze a person's current skill set and recommend courses, articles and resources that will help them acquire new competencies efficiently. By focusing on targeted skill development, individuals can increase their expertise in areas that directly contribute to their career advancement and financial growth. This targeted approach saves time and effort compared to more generalized learning methods.

Predictive Insights for Business Growth

For entrepreneurs and business owners, AI can offer predictive insights that guide strategic decisions. AI can analyze customer data, market trends and competitive landscapes to provide recommendations on product development, pricing strategies and marketing campaigns. This proactive approach to business management can lead to better results and ultimately, higher profits. Furthermore, AI can identify potential business risks and offer mitigation strategies. By addressing potential challenges before they escalate, individuals can avoid costly setbacks and disruptions, ensuring sustained growth with less effort expended on damage control.

Conclusion

The integration of AI technologies into our professional lives has the potential to transform how we work, allowing us to earn more while expending less effort. From automating routine tasks to optimizing time management and decision making, AI empowers individuals to focus on tasks that require human ingenuity and creativity. This, in turn, can lead to enhanced job satisfaction, improved work-life balance and increased financial success. However, it's important to acknowledge that while AI offers tremendous benefits, it's not a silver bullet. A healthy blend of human judgement, creativity and ethical considerations remains crucial for achieving true success. As individuals navigate the landscape of AI-driven productivity, they should keep in mind that the goal isn't just to work less, but to work smarter, making the most of AI's capabilities while preserving the human touch that is essential for meaningful and impactful work.

Augmenting Artistry with AI: A Path to Prosperity in Creative Fields

The convergence of AI and artistic expression is reshaping the landscape of creative industries. While art has historically been associated with inspiration and human intuition, AI is introducing new tools and techniques that can enhance artistic processes and propel creative professionals towards greater personal wealth. In this chapter I will show how AI is revolutionizing artistic fields, enabling individuals to leverage technology in ways that lead to increased financial success while preserving the core essence of human creativity.

Enhancing Creative Processes

AI technologies are empowering artists to push the boundaries of their creativity. Machine learning algorithms can analyze vast amounts of visual, audio and textual data to identify patterns, styles and trends. This enables artists to gain insights into audience preferences, helping them create content that resonates with their target demographic. For visual artists, AI tools can asist in generating initial sketches or mockups, reducing the time required to conceptualize ideas. Music composers and producers can utilize AI to create complex compositions and experiment with novel sound arrangements. Writers can employ AI-driven tools for idea generation, content optimization and even assistance in editing and proofreading.

Personalized Art Experiences

AI has introduced a new dimension to personalized art experiences. Artists can utilize AI algorithms to analyze individual preferences and behaviours, creating tailored content that resonates on a deeper level with their audience. For instance, museums and galleries can leverage AI to provide visitors with personalized audio tours or interactive exhibits that adapt to their interests in real-time. In the realm of digital art, non-fungible tokens (NFTs) have gained prominence as a way to monetize digital creations. AI can be use to generate unique NFTs that respond to different collector preferences, allowing artists to tap into new revenue streams within the digital art marketplace.

Expanding Market Reach

One of AI's most significant contributions to artistic fields is its ability to expand an artist's market reach. The digital age has made it possible for creators to share their work globally and AI can facilitate the discovery of artistic content by enhancing search algorithms and recommendation systems. Artists can use AI-driven platforms to gain exposure to wider audiences, resulting in increased visibility and potential sales. Social media platforms are ripe for AI integration. Algorithms can help artists identify optimal posting times, content themes and engagement strategies to maximize their online presence. This increased visibility can translate into higher demand for their work and consequently, greater financial success.

Collaboration and Innovation

AI can foster collaboration between artists and technologists, leading to innovative and groundbreaking creations. Artists can collaborate with AI experts to develop interactive installations, virtual reality experiences or generative artworks. This fusion of creativity and technology can attract attention from both art enthusiasts and tech-savvy audiences, driving demand and potential sales.

In the film and entertainment industry, AI-driven visual effects and animation tools can significantly reduce production timelines and costs. By automating certain processes, filmmakers can allocate resources to more critical aspects of production, resulting in higher quality content that resonates with audiences and generates revenue.

Intellectual Property and Monetization

AI introduces novel avenues for monetizing artistic creations. AI-generated content can be sold as digital products, such as stock images, music compositions and design templates. Artists can create AI-powered tools and assets that other creators can use, earning royalties with each sale. Additionally, AI can assist artists in protecting their intellectual property. With the rise of deepfake technology and AI-generated content, copyright infringement becomes a concern. AI tools can help artists detect unauthorized use of their work online, ensuring that they retain control over how their creations are used and monetized.

Conclusion

The marriage of AI and artistic expression is forging new possibilities for creatives seeking to increase their personal wealth while remaining true to their craft. AI's capacity to streamline creative processes, personalize art experiences, expand market reach, foster collaboration and enable new forms of monetization opens doors for artists in various fields to thrive financially.

It's important to recognize that AI is a tool that should be wielded thoughtfully and ethically. While AI can augment creativity, it cannot replace the inherent human touch and emotion that make art so compelling. As artists navigate the realm of AI-powered creativity, they have the opportunity to embrace technology as a means to enhance their personal wealth without sacrificing the authenticity and uniqueness that defines their work.

Empowering Economic Mobility: How AI can Elevate Low-Skilled Workers to Prosperity

The rise of AI has ignited discussions about its impact on the workforce. While concerns about job displacement are valid, AI also holds immense potential for elevating individuals with limited skills or higher education to greater economic prosperity. AI-driven tools and technologies can bridge the skills gap, create new pathways for career growth and empower low-skilled workers to tap into unprecedented opportunities for wealth accumulation. In the following pages I will explain how AI can be a catalyst for socio-economic mobility, enabling individuals to rise from low-skilled positions to financial success.

Democratizing Access to Education and Learning

AI-powered educational platforms have the potential to democratize access to learning and skill development. Online courses, tutorials and interactive modules driven by AI algorithms can cater to the learning needs of individuals with diverse backgrounds and skill levels. This inclusivity enables low-skilled workers to acquire new skills and knowledge that align with emerging job market demands. For example, AI-driven platforms can offer courses in digital literacy, data entry, basic programming and more, equipping individuals with the tools they need to thrive in a technology-driven economy. Such accessible learning resources empower individuals to augment their skill sets without the traditional barriers of time, location or financial resources.

Enhancing Task Automation and Efficiency

AI's capabilities extend to the automation of routine and manual tasks that have traditionally characterized low-skill jobs. By eliminating repetitive tasks, workers can transition to roles that require higher order skills and critical thinking. This not only increases their job satisfaction but also positions them for career advancement and higher earning potential. In industries like manufacturing, AI-powered robotics and automation streamline production processes, reducing the need for manual labor. Workers in these industries can shift from repetitive assembly line jobs to roles focused on maintaining and overseeing the AI-powered systems, enhancing their skill profiles and financial prospects.

Navigating the Gig Economy

The gig economy, characterized by short term contracts and freelance work, offers a new realm of opportunities for low-skilled workers to leverage. AI technologies, AI-powered platforms connect freelancers to job opportunities that match their skills, enabling them to monetize their abilities on a flexible schedule. Individuals with skills ranging from data entry and basic design to content creation and virtual assistance can tap into these platforms to earn income. Additionally, AI-driven gig platforms can provide personalized recommendations based on a worker's expertise and preferences, helping them secure projects that align with their strengths. This tailored approach increases the likelihood of success and financial gain in the gig economy.

Fostering Entrepreneurship and Innovation

AI is a powerful tool for fostering entrepreneurship and innovation, allowing individuals to create value-added services and products that cater to specific needs. Low-skilled workers can identify gaps in their communities or industries and develop AI-driven solutions to address them. For instance, individuals with limited education can create local service platforms powered by AI, connecting people seeking services with those willing to provide them. This concept can be applied to fields like household services, small-scale repairs or transportation solutions. By utilizing AI's capabilities to match demand and supply efficiently, entrepreneurs can generate income while filling critical gaps in the market.

Leveraging Data and Analytics

AI's ability to process and analyze vast amounts of data can empower low-skilled workers to make data-driven decisions and recommendations. This skill is increasingly valued in various industries, from retail to customer service. By understanding consumer behaviours and preferences through data analysis, workers can optimize sales strategies, enhance customer experiences and contribute to revenue growth. For example, workers in retail can use AI-driven analytics to predict consumer trends and adjust inventory levels accordingly. This proactive approach can lead to higher sales and profits, enabling workers to achieve financial success within their roles.

Conclusion

The transformative potential of AI is not confined to the realms of higher education and skilled labor; it holds the promise of uplifting low-skilled workers and individuals with limited educational backgrounds to financial prosperity. AI-driven learning platforms, task automation, gig economy opportuntities, entrepreneurship and data analytics all contribute to expanding the horizons for these individuals. As AI continues to advance, governments, educational institutions and businesses must collaborate to ensure that low-skilled workers have access to AI-driven learning resources and tools. Policies that support reskilling, upskilling and providing access to AI-driven technologies can empower individuals to embrace the potential of AI and chart a path towards wealth accumulation and a brighter economic future. The convergence of AI and human potential offers a remarkable opportunity to bridge the socio-economic divide and create a more inclusive and prosperous society.

From $1000 to $1 Million: A Strategic Blueprint Leveraging AI for Wealth Growth

Is it possible to grow $1000 into $1 million? Obviously this is an ambitious financial goal that requires careful planning, disciplined execution and strategic decision making. But by leveraging the power of AI, you can significantly enhance your chances of success. In this plan I will outline a step-by-step approach to help you achieve this goal by harnessing AI-driven investment strategies, skill development and entrepreneurial ventures.

Education and Skill Development

Invest in your knowledge and skill set as a foundational step. While AI can aid in wealth growth, understanding how it works and how to leverage it effectively is essential.

Online AI Courses: Begin by enrolling in online AI courses. Platforms like Coursera, edX and Khan Academy offer comprehensive courses that introduce you to the fundamentals of AI, machine learning and data analytics.

Data Analysis Skills: Acquire proficiency in data analysis. AI relies heavily on data and the ability to analyze and interpret data patterns will be crucial. Learn to use data analysis tools such as Python, R or specialized software like Tableau.

Financial Literacy: Deepen your understanding of finance and investment principles. Familiarize yourself with concepts such as risk management, portfolio diversification and market analysis.

1. AI-Driven Investment Strategy

An AI-driven investment strategy will play a pivotal role in growing your wealth. Consider the following steps:

Robo-Advisors: Utilize robo-advisory platforms that leverage AI algorithms to create and manage investment portfolios. Platforms like Betterment, Wealthfront and Acorns use data-driven insights to optimize your investment choices based on your risk tolerance and financial goals.

Automated Trading: Explore AI-driven automated trading platforms. These platforms use AI to analyze market trends, execute trades and manage your investments in real-time. Be cautious and thoroughly research the platform's performance and reputation before using this approach.

AI-Powered Stock Analysis: Leverage AI-powered tools for stock analysis. Platforms like AlphaSense and Kensho provide data-driven insights and predictions that can help you make informed decisions when trading stocks.

2. Gig Economy and Freelancing

Generating additional income through gig economy opportunities can accelerate your wealth growth. AI can help you find suitable gigs and enhance your skills to offer high demand services.:

Freelance Platforms: Join freelance platforms like Upwork, Freelancer or Fiverr to offer services that match your skills. Use AI-powered job matching tools to identify gigs that align with your expertise.

AI-Enhanced Skills: Hone your skills in fields where AI complements human capabilities. For instance, offer content creation, social media management or graphic design services and use AI tools to improve the quality and efficiency of your work.

3. Entrepreneurial Ventures

AI-driven innovations and startups provide unique opportunities for substantial wealth growth. Consider these steps to enter the entrepreneurial arena:

Identify Market Gaps: Research industries where AI has the potential to disrupt traditional models. Look for gaps in the market that AI-powered solutions could address more effectively.

Innovative Solutions: Develop AI-powered products or services that cater to emerging needs. Consider areas such as health, tech, fintech, sustainability or consumer experiences.

Collaboration: Collaborate with AI experts and developers to create innovative solutions. Building a multidisciplinary team ensures a comprehensive approach to solving complex problems.

4. Continuous Learning and Adaptation

The AI landscape is ever evolving, so staying informed and adaptable is crucial.

Stay Updated: Continuously update your knowledge of AI advancements, investment trends and entrepreneurial opportunities. Regularly follow reputable sources, attend conferences and participate in online forums and communities.

Network: Connect with professionals and experts in AI, finance and entrepreneurship. Networking can provide valuable insights, partnerships and opportunities that align with your wealth growth objectives.

Adaptation: Be prepared to adjust your strategies based on market changes, technological advancements and economic shifts. Flexibility and adaptability are key traits in a dynamic environment.

Conclusion

Growing $1000 to $1 million using AI requires a holistic approach that integrates education, investment strategies, gig economy opportunities and entrepreneurial ventures. By continuously improving your AI knowledge, investing wisely, leveraging AI-powered tools for income generation and innovating within the AI landscape, you can significantly enhance your potential to achieve this ambitious goal. However, remember that all investments carry inherent risks and it's essential to conduct thorough research and seek professional advice when needed. The journey to wealth requires dedication, discipline and a commitment to continuous learning and growth.

Unleashing Wealth through AI Advancements: Pioneering Opportunities for a Prosperous Future

The rapid and relentless revolution of AI has ignited a transformative revolution across industries, reshaping the way we work, communicate and conduct business. While the impacts of AI are already evident, its continuing development promises an even more profound influence on the global economy. Here I will explore how the ongoing advancement of AI is poised to create unprecedented opportunities for individuals to increase their wealth, propelling society into a new era of prosperity.

Unleashing Innovation and Entrepreneurship

AI's revolution is fueling an era of unparalleled innovation, offering fertile ground for entrepreneurs to sow the seeds of groundbreaking ideas and ventures. As AI technologies become more accessible and affordable, individuals with creative vision can harness these tools to develop novel solutions that address complex challenges. Startups leveraging AI-powered solutions are disrupting traditional industries, ranging from healthcare to finance, transportation and beyond. Entrepreneurs can create AI-driven products and services that streamline processes, enhance customer experiences and uncover untapped markets. The potential for substantial financial gains is significant, as these innovations can swiftly gain traction, capturing market share and generating lucrative opportunities for the creators.

Augmenting Human Skills and Expertise

The symbiotic relationship between humans and AI presents a paradigm shift in how tasks are performed and decisions are made. AI's capacity to process massive datasets and extract insights at lightening speed allows individuals to make more informed choices and predictions across domains. Professionals in fields such as finance, medicine, law and marketing can utilize AI to analyze complex information and patterns. For instance, AI-powered data analytics can aid investment decisions by identifying market trends and potential opportunities. In medicine, AI can assist doctors in diagnosing diseases by processing medical imaging data. This augmentation of human expertise translates to higher efficiency, accuracy and value creation, ultimately leading to financial rewards.

Revolutionizing Industries and Creating New Markets

AI's transformative potential extends beyond optimizing existing processes; it has the capacity to revolutionize industries and forge entirely new markets. As AI technologies continue to advance, they open doors to industries that were previously untapped or underdeveloped. For example, the autonomous vehicle industry is projected to reshape transportation and mobility, generating wealth through the development, manufacturing and deployment of self-driving cars. Similarly, the fusion of AI with renewable energy can create new opportunities in the clean energy sector, revolutionizing power generation, storage and distribution.

Personalizing Consumer Experiences

The seamless integration of AI into everyday life is shaping the future of consumer experiences. AI-driven personalization algorithms analyze individual preferences, behaviours and histories to deliver tailored products, services and content. This trend enhances customer satisfaction, driving engagement and subsequently, boosting revenue. E-commerce platforms, for example, employ AI to suggest products to customers based on their browsing history and past purchases. Streaming services use AI to curate playlists and recommend shows and movies that align with users' tastes. These personalized experiences not only improve customer loyalty but also increase the likelihood of repeat purchases and expanded market reach.

Expanding Gig Economy and Remote Work

The evolution of AI is reshaping the way work is performed, leading to the expansion of the gig economy and remote work opportunities. AI-powered platforms connect freelancers and remote workers with clients seeking specialized services, enabling individuals to monetize their unique skills from anywhere in the world. Professionals can participate in freelance projects that match their expertise, contributing to multiple projects simultaneously and diversifying income streams. Moreover, AI-powered tools facilitate remote collaboration, ensuring that individuals can work efficiently and seamlessly with teams located across different geographical locations.

AI as a Tool for Wealth Management

The ongoing development of AI is also making waves in personal finance and wealth management. AI-driven robo advisors analyze financial goals, risk tolerance and market conditions to create customized investment portfolios. These platforms offer accessible and cost-effective investment solutions that can generate wealth over time. Moreover, AI-powered financial management apps help individuals track their spending patterns, set budgets and optimize savings strategies. By leveraging AI to make informed financial decisions, individuals can maximize their savings and investment returns, leading to increased wealth accumulation.

Conclusion

The rapid evolution of AI is rewriting the playbook for wealth creation, offering individuals unpecedented opportunities to thrive in a rapidly changing world. From fostering innovation and entrepreneurship, to augmenting human skills, creating new markets, personalizing consumer experiences and revolutionizing work dynamics, AI's impact is both multfaceted and profound. However, while the prospects of AI are bright, it is essential to navigate its integration thoughtfully. Ethical considerations, regulation and the potential for job displacement, necessitate a balanced approach to harnessing AI's capabilities.

As AI continues to advance, individuals who proactively embrace these transformative technologies will find themselves at the forefront of new wealth-generating avenues. By staying curious, adaptive and open to innovation, individuals can position themselves to seize the multitude of opportunities that AI is poised to unfold, contributing to their personal prosperity and the broader advancement of society.

www.ingramcontent.com/pod-product-compliance
Lightning Source LLC
Chambersburg PA
CBHW062253290526
45794CB00006B/2527